—— THE WISDOM OF ——

FULTON SHEEN

with an introduction by Matthew Kelly

BLUE SPARROW

North Palm Beach, Florida

BLUE
sparrow

Cover Art by Cameron Smith.
Venerable Fulton Sheen, 2020.
studiocameronsmith.com

Cover Design by Madeline Harris
Typeset by Ashley Wirfel

ISBN: 978-1-63582-166-6 (hardcover)
ISBN: 978-1-63582-167-3 (e-Book)

10 9 8 7 6 5 4 3 2

Printed in the United States of America

FIRST EDITION

INTRODUCTION:
A MAN OF VISION

IN EVERY PLACE AND TIME, God raises up men and women to meet the specific needs of his people. Fulton Sheen is a perfect example.

Sheen was a visionary in every sense of the word. What were the qualities that made him a visionary? He was bold. He was an innovator. He was a disruptor. He was not afraid to fail. He had contagious enthusiasm. He was a man of action. He was a strategic thinker. Beyond his towering intellect, he possessed the much rarer emotional intelligence. He was willing to take risks. He was inspirational. And he was a dreamer. He was able to look into the future, imagine something bigger and better in the future, and then return to the present and work tirelessly to make that envisioned future a reality. There is a lot of talk these days about game-changers. Fulton Sheen was the living embodiment of a game-changer.

These qualities could have been applied with great success to any area of life, but Fulton Sheen courageously accepted God's invitation to serve his people.

It was Fulton Sheen's visionary spirit that led him to prophetically recognize the central place television would play in every American home, and the role it would play to influence and form society in decades to come. That insight led him to grasp a central place for our faith on prime-time television. It was a monumental accomplishment. If we truly wish to understand how significant this feat was, we only need to consider that fifty years ago he placed Catholic communications fifty years ahead of the mass-media efforts of other Christians and indeed all other faiths. Today, Catholic communications are fifty years behind the efforts of our non-Catholic Christian brothers and sisters. With the passing of fifty years, we have lost one hundred years of ground that needs to be made up if we are to effectively communicate with the people of our own times.

The idea of an Archbishop on television was and remains perplexing to people. But it should not be. Sheen was intimately connected to the ways of Jesus, and he knew that Jesus' model of reaching people was to go to the people. Television provided him with a way to go to millions of people in every city across the United States every night.

Jesus went to the people. He didn't stand in a synagogue or church and expect the people to come to him. He met them where they were and led them, little by little, to where he was calling them to be. Sheen did the same thing. He based his ministry on Jesus' model. He went to the people in many ways, but primarily by leveraging the power of television.

Television would quickly become the primary medium for influencing public opinion, and therefore a powerful tool to educate and evangelize. Fulton Sheen saw that long before it happened and harnessed it for the life-giving message of the Gospel. He saw what television was going to be and how important it was to harness it for good, to share a message of hope and inspiration with as many people as possible. I was born too late to witness the Fulton Sheen phenomenon, but I wish I had. It was boldness itself.

From the early 1950s to the late 1960s, Archbishop Fulton Sheen dominated the airways. He was a man so captivating, intelligent, and humorous that with his simple chalkboard he could outperform *I Love Lucy* and *The Ed Sullivan Show* night after night.

In order to truly understand it, you need to consider the idea of a Catholic bishop being allowed to teach and preach and laugh and joke on mainstream television during evening prime time. We live in an age where that would never happen. Sadly.

It was genius. Television allowed the beloved Fulton Sheen to meet people where they were literally, figuratively, and spiritually . . . and to inspire them to take one step closer to God with each encounter.

What was his message? "Life is worth living!" he proclaimed over and over again. At a time warped by the confusion of war and communism, the onset of new plagues of hedonism and materialism, he provided piercing clarity on matters large and small. Helping millions of people make the journey from confusion to clarity is an extraordinary contribution unto itself. He taught in ways that were practical and hopeful, and we all need a little practical advice from time to time that fills our hearts with the hope we need to walk the next mile of our journey.

Fulton Sheen was one of the greatest communicators to ever live and was literally the face of Catholicism in the United States for forty years.

In this beautiful collection of inspiring quotes from Sheen's life and works, we are given a unique glimpse into the heart, mind, and soul of this incredible man. With each turn of the page, it is easy to see why his inspiring and practical messages inspired so many during his lifetime and continue to inspire so many people today.

The Wisdom of Fulton Sheen is a powerful collection of writings that will encourage you to think differently about who you are, how your life is unfolding, what God is calling you to next, and what priorities will lead you to the peace and purpose you desire.

Sooner or later we all rise or fall to the level of our friendships. Invite Fulton Sheen deep into your life, make him one of your trusted friends, and he will elevate many aspects of your life.

His message was timely and timeless. This becomes quickly apparent as we read and reflect on the ideas he shares with us in these pages.

His contribution is incalculable. It is literally impossible to even guess how many people's lives were improved because this man walked the earth. It is equally impossible to calculate how many men, women, and children came to know God and his Church because Fulton Sheen laid down his life to serve others. May God give us ten more with his spirit – and give them to us soon.

I would like to close my reflection on this great man and his life of ministry with a lesson we can draw from his work that is of particular importance today.

What did Fulton Sheen do? Many things. What did his words and life accomplish? Many things. But there is one thing he did that is often overlooked. One thing that is central to his success that has been long ignored. He made people feel good about being Catholic. People were proud to be Catholic when Fulton Sheen was on television. They had someone, a national figure, that they could point to and say, "He's our guy."

What percentage of Catholics today do you think feel good about being Catholic? Are proud to be Catholic when the Church is mentioned in social conversation?

It may seem small or even trivial, but I promise you it is not. It is foundational, fundamental. It may be the late great Fulton Sheen's greatest lesson to us today.

The Catholic Church has fallen upon very difficult times today. How will we find our way forward? Where do we go from here? What is the answer to our paralyzing predicament? These are all important questions and we should be bringing the best minds of our times together to answer them and devise a plan. But I promise you this. Leading people to a place where they can feel good about being Catholic again is indispensable if we are going to forge a path forward for Catholics and the Church. Give them reason to be proud to be Catholic again, and they will move mountains.

People don't do anything until they are inspired. But once they are inspired, there is almost nothing they can't do. Fulton Sheen inspired people, and in doing so, he filled them with the courage to chase down and celebrate their God-given potential in a thousand different ways.

I hope he does the same for you.

— MATTHEW KELLY

JANUARY

JANUARY 1

The basic reason for loneliness is that man today has divorced himself from both love of God and love of neighbor.

JANUARY 2

Patience is power. Patience is not an absence of action; rather it is "timing" it waits on the right time to act, for the right principles and in the right way.

JANUARY 3

Broken things are precious. We eat broken bread because we share in the depth of our Lord and His broken life. Broken flowers give perfume. Broken incense is used in adoration. A broken ship saved Paul and many other passengers on their way to Rome. Sometimes the only way the good Lord can get into some hearts is to break them.

JANUARY 4

Criticism of others is thus an oblique form of self-commendation. We think we make the picture hang straight on our wall by telling our neighbors that all his pictures are crooked.

JANUARY 5

If you don't behave as you believe, you will end by believing as you behave.

JANUARY 6

Unless there is a Good Friday in your life, there can be no Easter Sunday.

JANUARY 7

Far better it is for you to say: "I am a sinner," than to say: "I have no need of religion." The empty can be filled, but the self-intoxicated have no room for God.

JANUARY 8

You must remember to love people and use things, rather than to love things and use people.

JANUARY 9

Never forget that there are only two philosophies to rule your life: the one of the cross, which starts with the fast and ends with the feast. The other of Satan, which starts with the feast and ends with the headache.

JANUARY 10

The refusal to take sides on great moral issues is itself a decision. It is a silent acquiescence to evil. The Tragedy of our time is that those who still believe in honesty lack fire and conviction, while those who believe in dishonesty are full of passionate conviction.

JANUARY 11

Once you have surrendered yourself, you make yourself receptive. In receiving from God, you are perfected and completed.

JANUARY 12

We become like that which we love. If we love what is base, we become base; but if we love what is noble, we become noble.

JANUARY 13

Show me your hands. Do they have scars from giving? Show me your feet. Are they wounded in service? Show me your heart. Have you left a place for divine love?

JANUARY 14

Nothing ever happens in the world that does not happen first inside human hearts.

JANUARY 15

Why are those who are notoriously undisciplined and unmoral also most contemptuous of religion and morality? They are trying to solace their own unhappy lives by pulling the happy down to their own abysmal depths.

JANUARY 16

Broadmindedness, when it means indifference to right and wrong, eventually ends in a hatred of what is right.

JANUARY 17

Jealousy is the tribute mediocrity pays to genius.

JANUARY 18

If you do not worship God, you worship something, and nine times out of ten it will be yourself. You have a duty to worship God, not because He will be imperfect and unhappy if you do not, but because you will be imperfect and unhappy.

JANUARY 19

The egocentric is always frustrated, simply because the condition of self-perfection is self-surrender. There must be a willingness to die to the lower part of self, before there can be a birth to the nobler.

JANUARY 20

There are two ways of waking up in the morning. One is to say, 'Good morning, God,' and the other is to say, 'Good God, morning'!

JANUARY 21

Christianity, unlike any other religion in the world, begins with catastrophe and defeat. Sunshine religions and psychological inspirations collapse in calamity and wither in adversity. But the Life of the Founder of Christianity, having begun with the Cross, ends with the empty tomb and victory.

JANUARY 22

As all men are touched by God's love, so all are also touched by the desire for His intimacy. No one escapes this longing; we are all kings in exile, miserable without the Infinite. Those who reject the grace of God have a desire to avoid God, as those who accept it have a desire for God.

JANUARY 23

To value only what can be "sold" is to defile what is truly precious. The innocent joy of childhood, the devotedness of a wife, the self sacrificing service of a daughter—none of these have an earthly market. To reduce everything to the dirty scales of economic values is to forget that some gifts, like Mary's, are so precious that the heart that offers them will be praised as long as time endures.

JANUARY 24

The world would hate His followers, not because of evil in their lives, but precisely because of the absence of evil or rather their goodness. Goodness does not cause hatred, but it gives occasion for hatred to manifest itself. The holier and purer a life, the more it would attract malignity and hate. Mediocrity alone survives.

JANUARY 25

The more you have, the more you are occupied, the less you give. But the less you have the more free you are. Poverty for us is a freedom. It is not mortification or penance. It is joyful freedom. There is no television here, no this, no that. But we are perfectly happy.

JANUARY 26

Love begins at home, and it is not how much we do . . . but how much love we put in that action.

JANUARY 27

Love cannot remain by itself—it has no meaning. Love has to be put into action, and that action is service.

JANUARY 28

Curiously enough, it is a fear of how grace will change and improve them that keeps many souls away from God. They want God to take them as they are and let them stay that way. They want Him to take away their love of riches, but not their riches—to purge them of the disgust of sin, but not of the pleasure of sin.

JANUARY 29

Whenever man attempts to do what he knows to be the Master's will, a power will be given him equal to the duty.

JANUARY 30

Because God is full of life, I imagine each morning Almighty God says to the sun, "Do it again;" and every evening to the moon and the stars, "Do it again;"and every springtime to the daisies, "Do it again;" and every time a child is born into the world asking for curtain call, that the heart of the God might once more ring out in the heart of the babe.

JANUARY 31

The Christian soul knows it needs Divine Help and therefore turns to Him Who loved us even while we were yet sinners. Examination of conscience, instead of inducing morbidity, thereby becomes an occasion of joy. There are two ways of knowing how good and loving God is. One is by never losing Him, through the preservation of innocence, and the other is by finding Him after one has lost Him. Repentance is not self-regarding, but God-regarding. It is not self-loathing, but God-loving. Christianity bids us accept ourselves as we really are, with all our faults and our failings and our sins.

FEBRUARY

FEBRUARY 1

In all other religions, one has to be good to come to God—in Christianity one does not. Christianity might be described as a "come as you are" party. It bids us stop worrying about ourselves, stop concentrating on our faults and our failings, and thrust them upon the Saviour with a firm resolve of amendment.

FEBRUARY 2

Love burdens itself with the wants and woes and losses and even the wrongs of others.

FEBRUARY 3

Why is it that any time we speak of temptation we always speak of temptation as something that inclines us to wrong. We have more temptations to become good than we do to become bad.

FEBRUARY 4

Love is the key to the mystery. Love by its very nature is not selfish, but generous. It seeks not its own, but the good of others. The measure of love is not the pleasure it gives-that is the way the world judges it-but the joy and peace it can purchase for others.

FEBRUARY 5

Head knowledge is worthless, unless accompanied by submission of the will and right action.

FEBRUARY 6

You cannot always depend on prayers to be answered the way you want them answered but you can always depend on God. God, the loving Father often denies us those things which in the end would prove harmful to us. Every boy wants a revolver at age four, and no father yet has ever granted that request. Why should we think God is less wise? Someday we will thank God not only for what He gave us, but also for that which He refused.

FEBRUARY 7

Two classes of people make up the world: those who have found God, and those who are looking for Him – thirsting, hungering, seeking! And the great sinners came closer to Him than the proud intellectuals! Pride swells and inflates the ego; gross sinners are depressed, deflated and empty. They, therefore, have room for God. God prefers a loving sinner to a loveless 'saint'. Love can be trained; pride cannot. The man who thinks that he knows will rarely find truth; the man who knows he is a miserable, unhappy sinner, like the woman at the well, is closer to peace, joy and salvation than he knows.

FEBRUARY 8

Counsel involving right and wrong should never be sought from a man who does not say his prayers.

FEBRUARY 9

No soul ever fell away from God without giving up prayer. Prayer is that which establishes contact with Divine Power and opens the invisible resources of heaven. However dark the way, when we pray, temptation can never master us. The first step downward in the average soul is the giving up of the practice of prayer, the breaking of the circuit with divinity, and the proclamation of one's owns self sufficiency.

FEBRUARY 10

Grace does not work like a penny in a slot machine. Grace will move you only when you want it to move you, and only when you let it move you. The supernatural order supposes the freedom of the natural order, but it does not destroy it.

FEBRUARY 11

Skeptics always want miracles such as stepping down from the Cross, but never the greater miracle of forgiveness.

FEBRUARY 12

The humble, simple souls, who are little enough to see the bigness of God in the littleness of a Babe, are therefore the only ones who will ever understand the reason of His visitation. He came to this poor earth of ours to carry on an exchange; to say to us, as only the Good God could say: 'you give me your humanity, and I will give you my Divinity; you give me your time, and I will give you My eternity; you give me your broken heart, and I will give you Love; you give me your nothingness, and I will give you My all.

FEBRUARY 13

A divine trick has been played on the human heart as if a violin teacher gave his pupil an instrument with one string missing. God kept a part of man's heart in Heaven, so that discontent would drive him back again to Him Who is Eternal Life, All-Knowing Truth and the Abiding Ecstasy of Love.

FEBRUARY 14

As the mother knows the needs better than the babe, so the Blessed Mother understands our cries and worries and knows them better than we know ourselves.

FEBRUARY 15

The day that man forgets that love is identical with sacrifice, he will ask how a God of love could demand mortification and self-denial.

FEBRUARY 16

The sun which warms the plant can under other conditions also wither it. The rain which nourishes the flower can under other conditions rot it. The same sun shines upon mud that shines upon wax. It hardens the mud but softens the wax. The difference is not in the sun, but in that upon which it shines. The Divine Life which shines upon a soul that loves Him, softens it into everlasting life; that same Divine Life which shines upon the slothful soul, neglectful of God, hardens it into everlasting death.

FEBRUARY 17

Charity is to be measured, not by what one has given away, but by what one has left.

FEBRUARY 18

Love is a vicarious principle. A mother suffers for and with her sick child, as a patriot suffers for his country. No wonder that the Son of Man visited this dark, sinful, wretched earth by becoming Man—Christ's unity with the sinful was due to His love! Love burdens itself with the wants and woes and losses and even the wrongs of others.

FEBRUARY 19

God has given different gifts for different people. There is no basis for feeling inferior to another who has a different gift. Once it is realised that we shall be judged by the gift we have received, rather than the gift we have not, one is completely delivered from a false sense of inferiority.

FEBRUARY 20

How can one love self without being selfish? How can one love others without losing self? The answer is: By loving both self and neighbor in God. It is His Love that makes us love both self and neighbor rightly.

FEBRUARY 21

In order to love anyone with your whole heart, in order to be really peaceful, in order to be really wholehearted, you must go back again to God to recover the piece He has been keeping for you from all eternity.

FEBRUARY 22

Say to yourself over and over again regardless of what happens: "God loves me!" And then add: "And I will try to love Him!"

FEBRUARY 23

Eternity is without succession, a simultaneous possession of all joys. To those who live toward Eternity, it really is not something at the end; it is that which influences every moment of the now.

FEBRUARY 24

The proud man counts his newspaper clippings; the humble, his blessings.

FEBRUARY 25

Truth must be sought at all costs, but separate isolated truths will not do. Truth is like life; it has to be taken on its entirety or not at all. . . . We must welcome truth even if it reproaches and inconveniences us—even if it appears in the place where we thought it could not be found.

FEBRUARY 26

Imagine a large circle and in the center of it rays of light that spread out to the circumference. The light in the center is God; each of us is a ray. The closer the rays are to the center, the closer the rays are to one another. The closer we live to God, the closer we are bound to our neighbor; the farther we are from God, the farther we are from one another. The more each ray departs from its center, the weaker it becomes; and the closer it gets to the center, the stronger it becomes.

FEBRUARY 27

Each instinct and passion of man is amoral; it is only the abuse of these passions that makes them wrong. There is nothing wrong about hunger, but there is something wrong about gluttony; there is no sin in thirst, but there is a sin in drunkenness; there is nothing wrong with a man who seeks economic security, but there is something wrong with a man who is avaricious; there is nothing to be despised in knowledge, but there is something to be condemned in pride; there is nothing wrong with the flesh, but there is something wrong in the abuse of the flesh.

FEBRUARY 28

As Adam lost the heritage of union with God in a garden, so now Our Blessed Lord ushered in its restoration in a garden. Eden and Gethsemane were the two gardens around which revolved the fate of humanity. In Eden, Adam sinned; in Gethsemane, Christ took humanity's sin upon Himself. In Eden, Adam hid himself from God; in Gethsemane, Christ interceded with His Father; in Eden, God sought out Adam in his sin of rebellion; in Gethsemane, the New Adam sought out the Father and His submission and resignation. In Eden, a sword was drawn to prevent entrance into the garden and thus immortalizing of evil; in Gethsemane, the sword would be sheathed.

FEBRUARY 29

The deaf who deny they are deaf will never hear;
the sinners who deny there is sin deny thereby the
remedy of sin, and thus cut themselves off forever
from Him Who came to redeem.

MARCH

MARCH 1

The lover of God never knows the words "too much." Those who accuse others of loving God or religion too much really do not love God at all, nor do they know the meaning of love.

MARCH 2

To a great extent the world is what we make it. We get back what we give. If we sow hate, we reap hate; if we scatter love and gentleness we harvest love and happiness. Other people are like a mirror which reflects back on us the kind of image we cast. The kind person bears with the infirmities of others, never magnifies trifles, and avoids a spirit of fault finding.

MARCH 3

Why is there more joy in Heaven for the repentant sinner than for the righteous? Because God's attitude is not judgment but love. In judgment, one is not as joyful after doing wrong as before; but in love, there is joy because the danger and worry of losing that soul is past. He who is sick is loved more than he who is well, because he needs it more.

MARCH 4

You are infinitely precious because you are loved by God.

MARCH 5

The very word mercy is derived from the Latin, *miserum cor,* a sorrowful heart. Mercy is, therefore, a compassionate understanding of another's unhappiness.

MARCH 6

A person is merciful when he feels the sorrow and misery of another as if it were his own.

MARCH 7

Love itself starts with the desire for something good.

MARCH 8

As scientific truths put us in an intelligent relation with the cosmos, as historic truth puts us in temporal relation with the rise and fall of civilization, so does Christ put us in intelligent relation with God the Father; for He is the only possible Word by which God can address Himself to a world of sinners.

MARCH 9

No man is good unless he is humble; and humility is a recognition of truth concerning oneself. A man who thinks he is greater than he actually is is not humble, but a vain and boastful fool.

MARCH 10

In almost nine cases out of ten, those who have once had the Faith but now reject it, or claim that it does not make sense, are driven not by reasoning but by the way they are living.

MARCH 11

To those who rejected Him, righteousness would one day appear as a terrible justice; to the sinful men who accepted Him and allied themselves to His life, righteousness would show itself as mercy.

MARCH 12

Once a man ceases to be of service to his neighbor, he begins to be a burden to him.

MARCH 13

George Bernard Shaw once said, "It is a pity that youth has been wasted on the young." The contrary is true. It is no secret at all that the Good Lord knew that it was better to put the illusions of life at the beginning in order that as we grew closer to eternity, we might the better see the purpose of living.

MARCH 14

So it is when we measure ourselves by God, we fall infinitely short; and when we compare ourselves with many who have given us inspiration, we feel a deep sense of unworthiness. But behind it all, and despite all of this, there is the tremendous consciousness of the mercy of God. He did not call angels to be priests; He called men. He did not make gold the vessel for his treasure; He made clay. The motley group of Apostles that He gathered about Him became more worthy through his mercy and compassion.

MARCH 15

There are two ways of knowing how good God is: one is never to lose Him, and the other is to lose Him and then to find Him.

MARCH 16

It is not so much what people suffer that makes the world mysterious; it is rather how much they miss when they suffer. They seem to forget that even as children they made obstacles in their games in order to have something to overcome.

MARCH 17

Life's temptations come most often from that for which one has the greatest aptitude.

MARCH 18

Here is the answer, after all these years, to the mysterious words in the Gospel of the Incarnation which stated that Our Blessed Mother laid her "firstborn" in the manger. Did that mean that Our Blessed Mother was to have other children? It certainly did, but not according to the flesh. Our Divine Lord and Savior Jesus Christ was the unique Son of Our Blessed Mother by the flesh. But Our Lady was to have other children, not according to the flesh, but according to the spirit!

MARCH 19

Joy never comes to those who seek it. In the self-for-getting hour when we are touched by another's need and sacrifice for it, we suddenly find our soul aflame with glorious joy.

MARCH 20

His words even imply that philanthropy has deeper depths than is generally realized. The great emotions of compassion and mercy are traced to Him; there is more to human deeds than the doers are aware. He identified every act of kindness as an expression of sympathy with Himself.

MARCH 21

All kindnesses are either done explicitly or implicitly in His name, or they are refused explicitly or implicitly in His name.

MARCH 22

Truth never appeals to us unless it is personal.

MARCH 23

Humility does not mean a submissiveness, a passiveness, a willingness to be walked on, or a desire to live in the doghouse. Humility is a virtue by which we recognize ourselves as we really are, not as we would like to be in the eyes of the public; not as our press notices say we are, but as we are in the sight of God when we examine our conscience.

MARCH 24

In vain will the world seek for equality until it has seen all men through the eyes of faith. Faith teaches that all men, however poor, or ignorant, or crippled, however maimed, ugly, or degraded they may be, all bear within themselves the image of God, and have been bought by the precious blood of Jesus Christ. As this truth is forgotten, men are valued only because of what they can do, not because of what they are.

MARCH 25

It is possible to love more than we know. A simple person in good faith may have a greater love of God than a theologian and, as a result, a keener understanding of the ways of God with the heart than psychologists have.

MARCH 26

Sanctity means separation from the spirit of the world, with immersion in the activity of the world. Saints would be in the world, not of it; they would have no public relation boosters to publicize them; they would never ask for money; perhaps the one venture which would stand out most in their lives would be poverty of spirit.

MARCH 27

There were only two classes of people who heard the cry Christmas night: shepherds and wise men. Shepherds: those who know they know nothing. Wise men: those who know they do not know everything. Only the very simple and very learned discovered God—never the man with one book.

MARCH 28

God can do something with those who see what they really are and who know their need of cleansing but can do nothing with the man who feels himself worthy.

MARCH 29

Deferred joys purchased by sacrifice are always sweetest and most enduring.

MARCH 30

The more you are led by God's love, the more you become yourself and it is all done without ever losing your freedom.

MARCH 31

It is the possibility of saying 'no' which gives so much charm to the heart when it says 'yes.' A victory may be celebrated only on those fields in which a battle may be lost. Hence, in the divine order of things, God made a world in which a man and woman would rise to moral heights, not by that blind driving power which makes the sun rise each morning, but rather by the exercise of that freedom in which one may fight the good fight and enjoy the reward of victory—for no one shall be crowned unless he has struggled.

APRIL

APRIL 1

Our blessed Lord was hopeful about humanity. He always saw men the way He originally designed them. He saw through the surface, grime, and dirt to the real man underneath. He never identified a person with sin. He saw sin as something alien and foreign which did not belong to man. Sin had mastered man but he could be freed from it to be his real self. Just as every mother sees her own image and likeness on her child's face, so God always saw the divine image and likeness beneath us.

APRIL 2

The true notion is that the material universe is a sign or an indication of what God is. We look at the purity of the snowflake and we see something of the goodness of God. The world is full of poetry: it is sin which turns it into prose.

APRIL 3

He seeks us before we dream of seeking him; he knocks before we invite him in; he loves us before we respond.

APRIL 4

Truth does grow, but it grows homogeneously, like an acorn into an oak . . . The nature of certain things is fixed, and none more so than the nature of truth. Truth may be contradicted a thousand times, but that only proves that it is strong enough to survive a thousand assaults.

APRIL 5

We lose our souls not only by the evil we do but also by the good we leave undone.

APRIL 6

Let no one think he can be totally indifferent to God in this life and suddenly develop a capacity for Him at the moment of death.

APRIL 7

The basis of all disappointment is the disproportion between what we imagine or wish for to make us happy and what we actually possess.

APRIL 8

A character is made by the kind of thoughts a man thinks when alone, and a civilization is made by the kind of thoughts a man speaks to his neighbor.

APRIL 9

Solitude can be very rewarding and full of blessing because in the silence of the inner being, one finds God.

APRIL 10

What is the difference between work and play? Work has a purpose, play has none, but there must be time in life for purposeless things.

APRIL 11

An unsuffering Christ Who did not freely pay the debt of human guilt would be reduced to the level of an ethical guide.

APRIL 12

Our Blessed Lord used an illustration of this mystery, "You cannot understand the blowing of the wind, but you obey its laws and thus harness its force; so also with the Spirit. Obey the law of the wind, and it will fill your sails and carry you onward. Obey the law of the Spirit and you will know the new birth. Do not postpone relationship with this law simply because you cannot fathom its mystery intellectually.

APRIL 13

So when God pulls down the curtain on the drama of the world's redemption, He will not ask what part we played, but only how well we played the role assigned to us.

APRIL 14

Let those souls who think their work has no value recognize that by fulfilling their insignificant tasks out of a love of God, those tasks assume a supernatural worth. The aged who bear the taunts of the young, the sick crucified to their beds, the ignorant immigrant in the steel mill, the street cleaner and the garbage collector, the wardrobe mistress in the theater and the chorus girl who never had a line, the unemployed carpenter and the ash collector—all these will be enthroned above dictators, presidents, kings, and cardinals if a greater love of God inspires their humbler tasks than inspires those who play nobler roles with less love.

APRIL 15

Blessed finally are the poor in spirit intellectually. Blessed are the humble, and the teachable who like the Shepherds know they know nothing, or like the Wise Men who know they do not know everything.

APRIL 16

God does not always spare the good from grief. The Father spared not the Son, and the Son spared not the mother.

APRIL 17

He often chooses weak instruments in order that His power might be manifested; otherwise it would seem that the good was done by the clay, rather than by the Spirit.

APRIL 18

We shrink therefore from God, knowing that He wants to enrich our being, rather than our having—that He wishes to elevate our nature, not to submerge and lose it in trifles. He has called us to the superior vocation of being His children, of partaking of His nature, and of being related to Him as branches to a vine. Few of us completely want that elevation; it is our petty desire to have more,not to share the glory of being more.We want the poor shadows, not the light—the sparks, and not the sun—the arc, and not the circle.

APRIL 19

As the desire for the world and things increases in us, God makes less and less appeal. We hold back, our fists closed about our few pennies, and thus lose the fortune He holds out to us. That is why the initial step of coming to God is so hard. We cling to our nursery toys and lose the pearl of great price.

APRIL 20

The greatest inhumanity that can be ascribed to men is having an opportunity for doing good to others and doing nothing. The serious sin is not always one of commission, but omission.

APRIL 21

This is the choice before us: either try to revolutionize the world and break under it or revolutionize ourselves and remake the world.

APRIL 22

To every Christian . . . there comes the supreme moment when he must choose between temporal pleasure and eternal freedom. In order to save our souls, we must often run the risk of losing our bodies.

APRIL 23

To pass from sadness to joy requires a birth, a moment of travail and labor, for no one ever mounts to a higher level of life without death to the lower.

APRIL 24

"To do God's Will until death, that is the inner heart of all holiness.

APRIL 25

Humility is not self-contempt but the truth about ourselves coupled with a reverence for others; it is self-surrender to the highest goal.

APRIL 26

Physical idleness deteriorates the mind; spiritual idleness deteriorates the heart.

APRIL 27

A smile is laughter's whisper and has its roots in the soul.

APRIL 28

No man hates God without first hating himself.

APRIL 29

If you are really humble, if you realize how small you are and how much you need God, then you cannot fail.

APRIL 30

I am often asked, "After Mother Teresa who?" That will be no trouble. God will find someone who is more humble, more obedient, more faithful, someone with a deeper faith, and He will do still greater things through her.

MAY

MAY 1

When I stand up to talk, people listen to me; they will follow what I have to say. Is it any power of mine? Of course not. St. Paul says, 'What have you that you have not received and you who have received, why do you glory as if you had not?' But the secret of my power is that I have never in fifty-five years missed spending an hour in the presence of our Lord in the Blessed Sacrament. That's where the power comes from. That's where sermons are born. That's where every good thought is conceived.

MAY 2

Prayer begins by talking to God, but it ends by listening to Him. In the face of Absolute Truth, silence is the soul's language.

MAY 3

Believe the incredible and you can do the impossible.

MAY 4

Our Lord did not ask us to give up the things of earth, but to exchange them for better things.

MAY 5

Theological insights are gained not only from between two covers of a book, but from two bent knees before an altar. The Holy Hour becomes like an oxygen tank to revive the breath of the Holy Spirit in the midst of the foul and fetid atmosphere of the world.

MAY 6

God does not love us because we are valuable. We are valuable because God loves us.

MAY 7

Joy is the happiness of love—love aware of its own inner happiness. Pleasure comes from without, and joy comes from within, and it is, therefore, within reach of everyone in the world . . .

MAY 8

A man without God is not like a cake without raisins; he is like a cake without the flour and milk; he lacks the essential ingredients.

MAY 9

Fasting detaches you from this world. Prayer reattaches you to the next world.

MAY 10

Our happiest times are those in which we forget ourselves, usually in being kind to someone else. That tiny moment of self-abdication is an act of true humility: the man who loses himself finds himself and finds his happiness.

MAY 11

So the divine love is sacrificial love. Love does not mean to have and to own and to possess. It means to be had and to be owned and to be possessed. It is not a circle circumscribed by self, it is arms outstretched to embrace all humanity within its grasp.

MAY 12

Leisure is a form of silence, not noiselessness. It is the silence of contemplation such as occurs when we let our minds rest on a rosebud, a child at play, a Divine mystery, or a waterfall.

MAY 13

There are three rules of dealing with all those who come to us: 1. Kindness, 2. Kindness, 3. Kindness.

MAY 14

Joy is not the same as pleasure or happiness. A wicked and evil man may have pleasure, while any ordinary mortal is capable of being happy. Pleasure generally comes from things, and always through the senses; happiness comes from humans through fellowship. Joy comes from loving God and neighbor. Pleasure is quick and violent, like a flash of lightning. Joy is steady and abiding, like a fixed star. Pleasure depends on external circumstances, such as money, food, travel, etc. Joy is independent of them, for it comes from a good conscience and love of God.

MAY 15

Every man rejoices twice when he has a partner in his joy. He who shares tears with us wipes them away. He divides them in two, and he who laughs with us makes the joy double.

MAY 16

Our personal dispositions are as windowpanes through which we see the world either as rosy or dull. The way we color the glasses we wear is the way the world seems to us.

MAY 17

The only difference between a sinner and a saint is found in their attitude toward their sins—the one persisting in them; the others weep bitterly.

MAY 18

Heaven is a city on a hill, hence we cannot coast into it; we have to climb. Those who are too lazy to mount can miss its capture as well as the evil who refuse to seek it.

MAY 19

Oh, what greater assurance is there in all the world of the mercy of God? Lost sheep, prodigal sons, broken Magdalens, penitent Peters, forgiven thieves! Such is the rosary of Divine forgiveness.

MAY 20

Pleasure is of the body; joy is of the mind and heart.

MAY 21

You think you are having a good time, but time really is the greatest obstacle in the world to happiness, not only because it makes you take pleasures successively, but also because you are never really happy until you are unconscious of the passing of time.

MAY 22

It is God you are looking for. Your unhappiness is not due to your want of fortune, or high position, or fame, or sufficient vitamins; it is due not to want of something outside you, but to a want of something inside you.

MAY 23

You were made for perfect happiness. That is your purpose. No wonder everything short of God disappoints you.

MAY 24

Unfortunately, many have become so enamored of the gifts the Great Giver of Life has dropped on the roadway of life that they build their cities around the gift, and forget the Giver.

MAY 25

Begin with your own emptiness and seek Him who can fill it.

MAY 26

We must keep going at anything we do until we get our second wind. One enjoys a mountain-climb more after passing through the first mountain of discouraged exhaustion. One becomes more interested in a job or work after the first impulse to drop it has been overcome.

MAY 27

The love of noise and excitement in modern civilization is due in part to the fact that people are unhappy on the inside. Noise exteriorized them, distracts them, and makes them forget their worries for the moment. There is an unmistakable connection between an empty life and a hectic pace.

MAY 28

To make progress the world must have action, but it must also know why it is acting, and that requires thought, contemplation, and silence.

MAY 29

It doesn't take much time to become a saint, only much love.

MAY 30

A mirror is silent, yet it reflects forets, sunsets, flowers and faces. Great ascetic souls, given to years of meditation, have taken on a radiance and a beauty which are beyond the outlines of faces. They seem to reflect, like the mirror on the outside, the Christ they bear within.

MAY 31

Humility is not underestimating oneself, such as the talented singer denying that he can sing. Humility is truth, or seeing ourselves as we really are—not as we think we are, nor as the public believe us to be, or as our press notices us.

JUNE

JUNE 1

Here is a psychological suggestion for acquiring peace of soul. Never brag; never talk about yourself; never rush to first seats at table or in a theater; never lord it over others as if you were better than they.

JUNE 2

The modern tendency is toward the affirmation of the ego, the exaltation of selfishness, riding roughshod over others in order to satisfy our own self-centeredness. It certainly has not produced much happiness, for the more the ego asserts itself, the more miserable it becomes.

JUNE 3

By expanding our puny little self to the Infinite, we have made the true Infinity of God seem trivial.

JUNE 4

Our hatred of a person often decreases as we learn to know him better.

JUNE 5

Pride is the child of ignorance, humility the offspring of knowledge.

JUNE 6

Proud people think themselves to be better than they are, and when criticized always believe their neighbor is jealous or has a grudge against them. The humble know themselves as they really are, for they judge themselves as they judge time, by a standard outside themselves, namely, God and His Moral Law.

JUNE 7

Humble people are not rigid exacters of things to which they have no undoubted right; they are always ready to overlook the faults of others, knowing that they have so many themselves.

JUNE 8

Desire is to the soul what gravitation is to matter. When we know our desires, we know the direction our soul is taking. If desire is heavenly, we go upwards. If it is wholly earthly, we go downwards. Desire is like raw material out of which we fashion either our virtues or vices.

JUNE 9

Unless we put God between ourselves and our previous life, we cannot hope to make real spiritual progress.

JUNE 10

If we revolve about what happens on the outside, then the latter determines our mood and attitudes. But if we make what is external revolve around us, we can determine the amount of their influence. Either what is outside makes our moods, or our moods determine out outlook on what is outside us.

JUNE 11

Our humor and disposition are not so much the reflection of the weather or the wrong side of the bed, as they are the reflections of the state of our soul.

JUNE 12

Be mindful that a happy conscience makes a happy outlook on life, and an unhappy conscience makes us miserable on the inside and everyone else miserable on the outside.

JUNE 13

When our conscience bothers us, whether we admit it or not, we often try to justify it by correcting others, or by finding fault with them.

JUNE 14

Joy is rejoicing in another's progress. This is one of the rarest virtues and the last to be won. Too often the progress of others is regarded as stolen from self.

JUNE 15

Those who discipline themselves and tame the ego by little acts of self-denial have already prepared themselves to meet crosses from the outside; they have familiarized themselves with them, and the shock is less when they are thrust on their shoulders.

JUNE 16

There are only two things we can do with crosses—carry them or kick against them. We can merge them in God's plan for life and thus make them serve our inner peace and happiness, or we can stumble over them to the glen of weeping.

JUNE 17

To demand love is to lose love. A selfish heart creates its own vacuum.

JUNE 18

Truth is not something we invent; if we do, it is a lie; rather, truth is something we discover, like love.

JUNE 19

There are many who excuse themselves, saying that if they were in other circumstances they would be much more patient. This is a grave mistake, for it assumes that virtue is a matter of geography, and not of moral effort.

JUNE 20

What happens to us is not as important, but rather how we react to what happens.

JUNE 21

Patience is the great remedy against becoming panicky. To be able to use reason and good judgment when everyone else goes to pieces not only saves self, but also neighbor.

JUNE 22

One of the greatest mistakes is to think that contentment comes from something outside us rather than from a quality of soul.

JUNE 23

Contentment, therefore, comes in part from faith—that is, from knowing the purpose of life and being assured that whatever the trails are, they come from the hand of a loving Father.

JUNE 24

In order to have contentment, one must also have a good conscience. If the inner self is unhappy because of moral failures and unatoned guilt, then nothing external can give rest to the spirit.

JUNE 25

A contented man is never [really] poor though he may have very, very little.

JUNE 26

Joy is the delightful experience of the feelings of pleasure at a good gained and actually enjoyed, or the prospect of good which one has a reasonable hope of obtaining.

JUNE 27

Spiritual joy is a serenity of temper in the midst of the changes of life, such as a mountain has when a storm breaks over it.

JUNE 28

No man can be happy on the outside who is already unhappy on the inside. If a sense of guilt weighs down the soul, no amount of pleasure on the outside can compensate for the loss of joy on the inside.

JUNE 29

If joy be uncommon today, it is because there are timid souls who have not the courage to forget themselves and to make sacrifices for their neighbor.

JUNE 30

Hunger is not just an economic problem. It is a moral and spiritual problem.

JULY

JULY 1

The reason most of us are what we are—mediocre Chrtisians, "up" one day, "down" the next—is simply because we refuse to let God work on us.

JULY 2

We always make the fatal mistake of thinking that it is what we do that matters, when really what matters is what we let God do to us."d contemplation must not be lived as a form of self-absorption; it must enlarge your heart to embrace all humanity, especially those who suffer.

JULY 3

God will love you, of course, even though you do not love Him, but remember, if you give Him only half your heart, He can make you only 50% happy.

JULY 4

You have freedom only to give [your heart] away. To whom do you give yours? You give it either to the moods, to the hour, to your egotism, to creatures, or to God.

JULY 5

The real test of a Chrstian is not how much he loves his friends, but now much he loves his enemies.

JULY 6

No man discovers anything big unless he makes himself small.

JULY 7

The Lord hears us more readily than we suspect; it is our listening to God that needs to be improved.

JULY 8

The essence of prayer is not the effort to make God give us something. Prayer, then, is not just informing God of our needs, for God already knows them. Rather, the purpose of prayer is to give God the opportunity to bestow the gifts He will give us when we are ready to accept them.

JULY 9

The person who thinks only of himself says only prayers of petition; the one who thinks of his neighbor says prayers of intercession; whoever thinks only of loving and serving God says prayers of abandonment to God's will, and this is the prayer of the saints.

JULY 10

It is never true to say that we have no time to meditate; the less one thinks of God, the less time there will always be for God. The time we have for anything depends of how much we value it.

JULY 11

Because he's born in a cave, all who wish to see him must be bend, must stoop, the stoop is the mark of humility. The proud refuse to stoop. Therefore they miss divinity. Those, however, who are willing to risk bending their egos to go into that cave, find that they are not in a cave at all; but they are in a universe where sits a babe on his mother's lap, the babe who made the world.

JULY 12

God walks into your soul with silent step. God comes to you more than you go to Him. Never will his coming be what you expect, and yet never will it disappoint. The more you respond to his gentle pressure, the greater will be your freedom.

JULY 13

Most of us do not like to look inside ourselves for the same reason we don't like to open a letter that has bad news.

JULY 14

Many souls fail to find God because they want a religion which will remake society without remaking themselves.

JULY 15

Help someone in distress and you lighten your own burden; the very joy of alleviating the sorrow of another is the lessening of one's own.

JULY 16

Most commit the same mistake with God that they do with their friends: they do all the talking.

JULY 17

Before the sin, Satan assures us that it is of no consequence; after the sin, he persuades us that it is unforgivable.

JULY 18

Nothing is more destined to create deep-seated anxieties in people than the false assumption that life should be free from anxiety.

JULY 19

It is easy to find truth, though it is hard to face it, and harder still to follow it.

JULY 20

You can quickly become tired of pleasures, but you can never tire of joys.

JULY 21

You want perfect life, and perfect truth, and perfect love. Nothing short of the Infinite satisfies you, and to ask you to be satisfied with less would be to destroy your nature . . . Why do you want Life, Truth, and Love unless you were made for them? How could you enjoy the fractions unless there were a whole?

JULY 22

Pleasure is best enjoyed when it comes to us as a "treat," in contrast to experiences that are less pleasurable. We make a great mistake if we try to have all our nights party-nights. No one would enjoy Thanksgiving if every meal were a turkey dinner. New Year's Event would not delight us if the whistles blew at midnight every night.

JULY 23

Self-discipline brings back to us the excitement of our childhood, when our pleasures were rationed—when we got our dessert at the end of the meal and never at the start.

JULY 24

We must leave the world to help the world. That life is most effectively lived which every now and then withdraws from the scene of action to contemplation, where one learns the terrible defeat and futility which comes from excessive absorption in detail and action.

JULY 25

In silence, there is humility of spirit or what might be called "wise passivity." In such the ear is more important than the tongue. God speaks, but not in cyclones—only in the zephyrs and gentle breezes.

JULY 26

Only in true solitariness is true spirituality born, when the soul stands naked before its God.

JULY 27

Though truth is not personal, we make it personal by contemplation.

JULY 28

We cannot get a real satisfaction out of our work unless we pause, frequently, to ask ourselves why we are doing it, and whether its purpose is one (of which) our minds wholeheartedly approve.

JULY 29

If we direct our work towards God, we shall work better than we know.

JULY 30

The humble are not cast down by the censures or the slights of others. If they have unconsciously given occasion for them, they amend their faults; if they deserve them not, they treat them as trifles.

JULY 31

By finding others who apparently are more evil than we, we falsely believe that we are somehow better "than the rest of men" (Luke 18:11). It used to be that the most popular biographies were stories about the lives of good men and women worthy of our imitation, rather than the recounting of scandals for the sake of making us believe we are more virtuous than we really are.

AUGUST

AUGUST 1

Before undertaking a task great or small, before making decisions, before beginning a journey, the humble will acknowledge their dependence on God and invoke His guidance and His blessing on all their enterprises.

AUGUST 2

There is a world of difference between submitting to the Divine Will from sullenness and submitting to it knowing that God is Supreme Wisdom, and that some day we will know all that happened, happened for the best.

AUGUST 3

There is a marvelous peace that comes into the soul if all trials and disappointments, sorrows and pains are accepted either as deserved chastisement for our sins, or as a healthful discipline which will lead us to greater virtue.

AUGUST 4

Contentment is not inconsistent with our endeavor to have our condition improved. We do everything we can, as if all depended on us, but we trust in God as if everything depended on him.

AUGUST 5

It does no good to blame the golf club if our game is at fault, or the pitcher because we spill the milk; the fault must be seen as our own in little mishaps of this kind, and for our states of mind as well. The discovery that we are to blame for being the way we are is greater than the discovery made by an explorer—such a discovery of our own fault is impossible unless there be a higher standard outside ourselves, from whose love we know we have fallen.

AUGUST 6

We begin to act differently when we recognize the immensity of our possibilities.

AUGUST 7

The new atheism is not of the intellect, but of the will; it is an act of free and eager rejection of morality and its demands. It starts with the affirmation of self and the denial of the moral law.

AUGUST 8

The modern world, which denies personal guilt, which has no place for personal repentance but only public reforms, has divorced Christ from His Cross; the Bridegroom and Bride have been pulled apart. What God hath joined together, men have torn asunder.

AUGUST 9

We hate others, and call it "zeal"; we flatter others because of what they can do for us, and call it "love"; we lie to them, and call it "tact."

AUGUST 10

Who is going to save our Church? Not our bishops, not our priests and religious. It is up to you, the people. You have the minds, the eyes, the ears to save the Church. Your mission is to see that your priests act like priests, your bishops like bishops, and your religious act like religious.

AUGUST 11

There are not one hundred people in the United States who hate The Catholic Church, but there are millions who hate what they wrongly perceive the Catholic Church to be.

AUGUST 12

Books are the most wonderful friends in the world. When you meet them and pick them up, they are always ready to give you a few ideas. When you put them down, they never get mad; when you take them up again, they seem to enrich you all the more.

AUGUST 13

Too many people get credit for being good, when they are only being passive. They are too often praised for being broadminded when they are so broadminded they can never make up their minds about anything.

AUGUST 14

A teacher who cannot explain any abstract subject to a child does not himself thoroughly understand his subject; if he does not attempt to break down his knowledge to fit the child's mind, he does not understand teaching.

AUGUST 15

America, it is said, is suffering from intolerance—it is not. It is suffering from tolerance. Tolerance of right and wrong, truth and error, virtue and evil, Christ and chaos. Our country is not nearly so overrun with the bigoted as it is overrun with the broadminded.

AUGUST 16

A man may stand for the justice of God, but a woman stands for His Mercy.

AUGUST 17

There are ultimately only two possible adjustments to life; one is to suit our lives to principles; the other is to suit principles to our lives. If we do not live as we think, we soon begin to think as we live. The method of adjusting moral principles to the way men live is just a perversion of the order of things.

AUGUST 18

Tolerance is an attitude of reasoned patience toward evil . . . a forbearance that restrains us from showing anger or inflicting punishment. Tolerance applies only to persons . . . never to truth. Tolerance applies to the erring, intolerance to the error . . . Architects are as intolerant about sand as foundations for skyscrapers as doctors are intolerant about germs in the laboratory. Tolerance does not apply to truth or principles. About these things we must be intolerant, and for this kind of intolerance, so much needed to rouse us from sentimental gush, I make a plea. Intolerance of this kind is the foundation of all stability.

AUGUST 19

God is a consuming fire; our desire for God must include a willingness to have the chaff burned from our intellect and the weeds of our sinful will purged. The very fear souls have of surrendering themselves to the Lord with a cross is an evidence of their instinctive belief in His Holiness. Because God is fire, we cannot escape Him, whether we draw near for conversion or flee from aversion: in either case, He affects us. If we accept His love, its fires will illumine and warm us; if we reject Him, they will still burn on in us in frustration and remorse.

AUGUST 20

Each of us makes his own weather, determines the color of the skies in the emotional universe which he inhabits.

AUGUST 21

Moral principles do not depend on a majority vote. Wrong is wrong, even if everybody is wrong. Right is right, even if nobody is right.

AUGUST 22

We are all born with the power of speech, but we need grammar. Conscience, too, needs Revelation.

AUGUST 23

The evil in the world must not make me doubt the existence of God. There could be no evil if there were no God. Before there can be a hole in a uniform, there must be a uniform; before there is death, there must be life; before there is error, there must be truth; before there is a crime, there must be liberty and law; before there is a war, there must be peace; before there is a devil, there must be a God, rebellion against whom made the devil.

AUGUST 24

Why did Our Blessed Lord use bread and wine as the elements of this Memorial? First of all, because no two substances in nature better symbolize unity than bread and wine. As bread is made from a multiplicity of grains of wheat, and wine is made from a multiplicity of grapes, so the many who believe are one in Christ. Second, no two substances in nature have to suffer more to become what they are than bread and wine. Wheat has to pass through the rigors of winter, be ground beneath the Calvary of a mill, and then subjected to purging fire before it can become bread. Grapes in their turn must be subjected to the Gethsemane of a wine press and have their life crushed from them to become wine. Thus, do they symbolize the Passion and Sufferings of Christ, and the condition of Salvation, for Our Lord said unless we die to ourselves we cannot live in Him.

AUGUST 25

The nearer Christ comes to a heart, the more it becomes conscious of its guilt; it will then either ask for his mercy and find peace, or else it will turn against Him because it is not yet ready to give up its sinfulness. Thus He will separate the good from the bad, the wheat from the chaff. Man's reaction to this Divine Presence will be the test: either it will call out all the opposition of egotistic natures, or else galvanize them into a regeneration and a resurrection.

AUGUST 26

Those who think they are healthy but have a hidden moral cancer are incurable; the sick who want to be healed have a chance. All denial of guilt keeps people out of the area of love and, by inducing self-righteousness, prevents a cure. The two facts of healing in the physical order are these: A physician cannot heal us unless we put ourselves into his hands, and we will not put ourselves into his hands unless we know that we are sick. In like manner, a sinner's awareness of sin is one requisite for his recovery; the other is his longing for God. When we long for God, we do so not as sinners, but as lovers.

AUGUST 27

The worldly are willing to let anyone believe in God if he pleases, but only on condition that a belief in God will mean no more than belief in anything else. They will allow God, provided that God does not matter. But taking God seriously is precisely what makes the saint.

AUGUST 28

Wars come from egotism and selfishness. Every macrocosmic or world war has its origin in microcosmic wars going on inside millions and millions of individuals.

AUGUST 29

"But there was no room at the inn"; the inn is the gathering place of public opinion; so often public opinion locks its doors to the King.

AUGUST 30

A dying man asked a dying man for eternal life; a man without possessions asked a poor man for a Kingdom; a thief at the door of death asked to die like a thief and steal Paradise. One would have thought a saint would have been the first soul purchased over the counter of Calvary by the red coins of Redemption, but in the Divine plan it was a thief who was the escort of the King of kings into Paradise. If Our Lord had come merely as a teacher, the thief would never have asked for forgiveness. But since the thief's request touched the reason of His coming to earth, namely, to save souls, the thief heard the immediate answer.

AUGUST 31

It was the thief's last prayer, perhaps even his first. He knocked once, sought once, asked once, dared everything, and found everything. When even the disciples were doubting and only one was present at the Cross, the thief owned and acknowledged Him as Savior.

SEPTEMBER

SEPTEMBER 1

Since the basic cause of man's anxiety is the possibility of being either a saint or a sinner, it follows that there are only two alternatives for him. Man can either mount upward to the peak of eternity or else slip backwards to the chasms of despair and frustration. Yet there are many who think there is yet another alternative, namely, that of indifference. They think that, just as bears hibernate for a season in a state of suspended animation, so they, too, can sleep through life without choosing to live for God or against Him. But hibernation is no escape; winter ends, and one is then forced to make a decision—indeed, the very choice of indifference is itself a decision. White fences do not remain white fences by having nothing done to them; they soon become black fences.

SEPTEMBER 2

A man who has taken poison into his system can ignore the antidote, or he can throw it out the window; it makes no difference which he does, for death is already on the march. By the mere fact that we do not go forward, we go backward. There are no plains in the spiritual life, we are either going uphill or coming down.

SEPTEMBER 3

The wicked fear the good, because the good are a constant reproach to their consciences. The ungodly like religion in the same way that they like lions, either dead or behind bars; they fear religion when it breaks loose and begins to challenge their consciences.

SEPTEMBER 4

Why are you disappointed? Because of the tremendous disproportion between your desires and your realizations. Your soul has a certain infinity about it, because it is spiritual. But your body, like the world around you, is material, limited, "cabined, cribbed, confined."

SEPTEMBER 5

In moments when fever, agony, and pain make it hard to pray, the suggestion of prayer that comes from merely holding the rosary—or better still, from caressing the Crucifix at the end of it—is tremendous!

SEPTEMBER 6

The fact the enemies of God must face is that modern civilization has conquered the world, but in doing so has lost its soul. And in losing its soul it will lose the very world it gained . . . And as religion fades so will freedom, for only where the spirit of God is, is there liberty.

SEPTEMBER 7

Love of self without love of God is selfishness; love of neighbor without love of God embraces only those who are pleasing to us, not those who are hateful.

SEPTEMBER 8

Conversion can also occur among those who already have the faith. Christians will become real Christians, with less façade and more foundation. Catastrophe will divide them from the world, force them to declare their basic loyalties; it will revive shepherds who shepherd rather than administrate, reverse the proportion of saints and scholars in favor of saints, create more reapers for the harvest, more pillars of fire for the lukewarm; it will make the rich see that real wealth is in the service of the needy; and, above all else, it will make the glory of Christ's Cross shine out in a love of the brethren for one another as true and loyal sons of God."

SEPTEMBER 9

Love of God thus becomes the dominant passion of life; like every other worth-while love, it demands and inspires sacrifice. But love of God and man, as an ideal, has lately been replaced by the new ideal of tolerance which inspires no sacrifice. Why should any human being in the world be merely tolerated? What man has ever made a sacrifice in the name of tolerance? It leads men, instead, to express their own egotism in a book or a lecture that patronizes the downtrodden group. One of the cruelest things that can happen to a human being is to be tolerated. Never once did Our Lord say, "Tolerate your enemies!" But He did say, "Love your enemies; do good to them that hate you" (Matt. 5:44). Such love can be achieved only if we deliberately curb our fallen nature's animosities.

SEPTEMBER 10

If we use our lives for other purposes than those given by God, not only do we miss happiness, but we actually hurt ourselves and beget in us queer little "kinks."

SEPTEMBER 11

It is not easy to explain why God permits evil; but it is impossible for an atheist to explain the existence of goodness. How could a spiritless, soul-less, cross-less, Godless universe become the center of faith, purity, sacrifice, and martyrdom? How can decency be the decent thing if there is no God? Since God is love, why should we be surprised that want of it should end in pain, hate, broken hearts, and war?

SEPTEMBER 12

Holiness must have a philosophical and theological foundation, namely, Divine truth; otherwise it is sentimentality and emotionalism. Many would say later on, 'We want religion, but no creeds.' This is like saying we want healing, but no science of medicine; music, but no rules of music; history, but no documents. Religion is indeed a life, but it grows out of truth, not away from it. It has been said it makes no difference what you believe, it all depends on how you act. This is psychological nonsense, for a man acts out of his beliefs. Our Lord placed truth or belief in Him first; then came sanctification and good deeds. But here truth was not a vague ideal, but a Person. Truth was now lovable, because only a Person is lovable. Sanctity becomes the response the heart makes to Divine truth and its unlimited mercy to humanity.

SEPTEMBER 13

The soul cannot be seen in a biological laboratory, any more than pain can be seen on an operating table.

SEPTEMBER 14

Modern prophets say that our economics have failed us. No! It is not our economics which have failed; it is man who has failed-man who has forgotten God. Hence no manner of economic or political readjustment can possibly save our civilization; we can be saved only by a renovation of the inner man, only by a purging of our hearts and souls; for only by seeking first the Kingdom of God and His Justice will all these other things be added unto us.

SEPTEMBER 15

The more He loved those for whom He was the ransom, the more His anguish would increase, as it is the faults of friends rather than enemies which most disturb hearts!

SEPTEMBER 16

Very harmful effects can follow accepting the philosophy which denies personal guilt or sin and thereby makes everyone nice. By denying sin, the nice people make a cure impossible. Sin is most serious, and the tragedy is deepened by the denial that we are sinners . . . The really unforgivable sin is the denial of sin, because, by its nature, there is now nothing to be forgiven. By refusing to admit to personal guilt, the nice people are made into scandalmongers, gossips, talebearers, and supercritics, for they must project their real if unrecognized guilt to others. This, again, gives them a new illusion of goodness: the increase of faultfinding is in direct ratio and proportion to the denial of sin.

SEPTEMBER 17

Unhappy souls almost always blame everyone but themselves for their miseries. Shut up within themselves, they are necessarily shut off from all others except to criticize them. Since the essence of sin is opposition to God's will, it follows that the sin of one individual is bound to oppose any other individual whose will is in harmony with God's will. This resulting estrangement from one's fellow man is intensified when one begins to live solely for this world, then the possessions of the neighbor are regarded as something unjustly taken from oneself. Once the material becomes the goal of life, a society of conflicts is born.

SEPTEMBER 18

He came to put a harlot above a Pharisee, a penitent robber above a High Priest, and a prodigal son above his exemplary brother. To all the phonies and fakers who would say that they could not join the Church because His Church was not holy enough, He would ask, 'How holy must the Church be before you will enter into it?' If the Church were as holy as they wanted it to be, they would never be allowed into it! In every other religion under the sun, in every Eastern religion from Buddhism to Confucianism, there must always be some purification before one can commune with God. But Our Blessed Lord brought a religion where the admission of sin is the condition of coming to Him. 'Those who are well have no need of a physician, but those who are ill.

SEPTEMBER 19

The good repent on knowing their sin; the evil become angry when discovered.

SEPTEMBER 20

If it be a terrible thing to fall into the hands of the living God,It is a more terrible thing to fall out of them.

SEPTEMBER 21

It was not enough that the Son of God should come down from the heavens and appear as the Son of Man, for then He would have been only a great teacher and a great example, but not a Redeemer. It was more important for Him to fulfill the purpose of the coming, to redeem man from sin while in the likeness of human flesh. Teachers change men by their lives; Our Blessed Lord would change men by His death. The poison of hate, sensuality, and envy which is in the hearts of men could not be healed simply by wise exhortations and social reforms. The wages of sin is death, and therefore it was to be by death that sin would be atoned for.

SEPTEMBER 22

If it be true that the world has lost its respect for authority, it is only because it lost it first in the home. By a peculiar paradox, as the home loses its authority, the authority of the state becomes tyrannical.

SEPTEMBER 23

Evil is thus a kind of parasite on goodness. If there were no good by which to measure things, evil could not exist. Men sometimes forget this, and say, there is so much evil in the world that there cannot be a God. They are forgetting that, if there were no God, they would have no way of distinguishing evil from goodness. The very concept of evil admits and recognizes a Standard, a Whole, a Rule, an Order. Nobody would say that his automobile was out of order if he did not have a conception of how an automobile ought to run.

SEPTEMBER 24

This figure upon the Cross is not a MVD agent or a Gestapo inquisitor, but a Divine Physician, Who only asks that we bring our wounds to Him in order that He may heal them. If our sins be as scarlet, they shall be washed white as snow, and if they be as red as crimson, they shall be made white as wool.

SEPTEMBER 25

The melody of her life is played just as it was written. Mary was thought, conceived, and planned as the equal sign between ideal and history, thought and reality, hope and realization.

SEPTEMBER 26

Conscience, Christ, and the gift of faith make evil men uneasy in their sin. They feel that if they could drive Christ from the earth, they would be free from "moral inhibitions." They forget that it is their own nature and conscience which makes them feel that way. Being unable to drive God from the heavens, they would drive his ambassadors from the earth. In a lesser sphere, that is why many men sneer at virtue—because it makes vice uncomfortable.

SEPTEMBER 27

To love what is below the human is degradation; to love what is human for the sake of the human is mediocrity; to love the human for the sake of the Divine is enriching; to love the Divine for its own sake is sanctity.

SEPTEMBER 28

He has mercy on those who fear Him, from generation to generation. Fear is here understood as filial, that is, a shrinking from hurting one who is loved. Such is the fear a son has for a devoted father and the fear a Christian has of Christ. Fear is here related to love.

SEPTEMBER 29

A man who makes himself a god must hide; otherwise his false divinity will be unmasked.

SEPTEMBER 30

Though the Son of Man expressed His federation with humanity, He was very careful to note that He was like man in all things save sin. He challenged His hearers to convict Him of sin. But the consequences of sin were all His as the Son of Man. Hence the prayer to let the chalice pass; His endurance of hunger and thirst; His agony and bloody sweat . . . His endurance of worry, anxiety, fear, pain, mental anguish, fever, hunger, thirst, and agony during the hours of His Passion—all these things were to inspire men to imitate the Son of Man. Nothing that was human was foreign to Him.

OCTOBER

OCTOBER 1

The Church knows too that to marry the present age and its spirit is to become a widow in the next.

OCTOBER 2

Weak men in high positions surround themselves with little men, in order that they may seem great by comparison.

OCTOBER 3

Two principles inspire much of the personal and social dealings of many a citizen in our land: "What can I get out of it?" and "Can I get away with it?" Evil is confused with good, and good is confused with evil. Revolting books against virtue are termed "courageous"; those against morality are advertised as "daring and forward-looking"; and those against God are called "progressive and epoch-making." It has always been the characteristic of a generation in decay to paint the gates of Hell with the gold of Paradise. In a word, much of the so-called wisdom of our day is made up of that which once nailed our blessed Lord to the Cross.

OCTOBER 4

Purity does not begin in the body but in the will. From there it flows outward, cleansing thought, imagination, and, finally, the body. Bodily purity is a repercussion or echo of the will. Life is impure only when the will is impure.

OCTOBER 5

What the new morality resolves itself into is this: You are wrong if you do a thing you do not feel like doing; and you are right if you do a thing you feel like doing. Such a morality is based not only on "fastidiousness," but on "facetiousness." The standard of morality then becomes the individual feeling of what is beautiful, instead of the rational estimate of what is right.

OCTOBER 6

The Old Testament begins with the Genesis of heaven and earth through God making all things. The New Testament had another kind of Genesis, in the sense that it describes the making of all things new.

OCTOBER 7

Politics has become so all-possessive of life, that by impertinence it thinks the only philosophy a person can hold is the right or the left. This question puts out all the lights of religion so they can call all the cats gray. It assumes that man lives on a purely horizontal plane, and can move only to the right or the left. Had we eyes less material, we would see that there are two other directions where a man with a soul may look: the vertical directions of "up" or "down."

OCTOBER 8

Animals never have recourse to law courts, because they have no will to love; but man, having reason, feels the need of justifying his irrational behavior when he does wrong.

OCTOBER 9

One would not generally put garbage into the stomach, but too often one will put garbage into the mind.

OCTOBER 10

As education, when it loses its philosophy of life, breaks up into departments without any integration or unity except the accidental one of proximity and time, and as a body, when it loses its soul, breaks up into its chemical components, so a family, when it loses the unifying bond of love, breaks up in the divorce court.

OCTOBER 11

We suffer from hunger of the spirit while much of the world is suffering from hunger of the body.

OCTOBER 12

In the Christian order, it is not the important who are essential, nor those who do great things who are really great. A king is no nobler in the sight of God than a peasant. The head of government with millions of troops at his command is no more precious in the sight of God than a paralyzed child. The former has greater opportunities for evil, but like the widow in the Temple, if the child fulfills his task of resignation to the will of God more than the dictator fulfills his task of procuring social justice for the glory of God, then the child is greater. By our presence in the world, we are called to create a society capable of recognizing the dignity of every person and sharing the gift that each person is to the other.

OCTOBER 13

One can well believe that a crown of thorns, and that steel nails were less terrible to the flesh of our Savior than our modern indifference which neither scorns nor prays to the Heart of Christ."

OCTOBER 14

Like train announcers, they know all the stations, but never travel. Head knowledge is worthless, unless accompanied by submission of the will and right action.

OCTOBER 15

It meant nothing to teach men to be good unless He also gave them the power to be good.

OCTOBER 16

Sensationalists miss divinity for just that reason: the true religion is always unspectacular. The foolish virgins go to buy oil for their lamps, and when they come back, they find the Bridegroom already returned. And the door closed. It was so undramatic. A beautiful maiden knocks at the door of an inn, and an innkeeper tells her there is no room. Into a stable she enters, and there a child is born. It was God's entrance into the world. But it was so undramatic.

OCTOBER 17

From my experience it is always well never to pay attention to what people say, but rather why they say it.

OCTOBER 18

Make this experiment whether you believe in God or not. At your first opportunity, stop in a Catholic Church for a visit. You need not believe, as we Catholics do, that Our Lord is really and truly present in the tabernacle. But just sit there for an hour, and within that hour you will experience a surpassing peace the like of which you never before enjoyed in your life. You will ask yourself as a sensationalist once asked me when we made an all-night vigil of adoration in the Basilica of Sacre Coeur in Paris: "What is it that is in that church?" Without voice or argument or thundering demands, you will have an awareness of something before which your spirit trembles—a sense of the Divine.

OCTOBER 19

Everyone else who was ever born into the world, came into it to live; our Lord came into it to die.

OCTOBER 20

If then Death was the supreme moment for which Christ lived, it was therefore the one thing He wished to have remembered. He did not ask that men should write down His Words into a Scripture; He did not ask that His kindness to the poor should be recorded in history; but He did ask that men remember His Death. And in order that it's memory might not be any hap-hazard narrative on the part of men, He Himself instituted the precise way it should be recalled. The memorial was instituted the night before He died, at what has since been called "The Last Supper." He was offering Himself as a Victim to be immolated, and that men might never forget that "greater love than this no man hath, that a man lay down his life for his friends," He gave the divine command to the Church: "Do this for a commemoration of me."

OCTOBER 21

Finite intelligence needs many words in order to express ideas; but God speaks once and for all within Himself—one single Word which reaches the abyss of all things that are known and can be known. In that Word of God are hidden all the treasures of wisdom, all the secrets of sciences, all the designs of the arts, all the knowledge of mankind. But this knowledge, compared to the Word, is only the feeblest broken syllable.

OCTOBER 22

Character is to some extent judged by what a man does with his falls. A pig falls into the mud and stays there; a sheep falls in and climbs out.

OCTOBER 23

Our intellects do not make the truth; they attain it: they discover it.

OCTOBER 24

Politeness is a way of showing externally the internal regard we have for others. Good manners are the shadows cast by virtues.

OCTOBER 25

Life is like a cash register, in that every account, every thought, every deed, like every sale, is registered and recorded.

OCTOBER 26

If, in his pride, he considers God as a challenge, he will deny Him; and if God becomes man and therefore makes Himself vulnerable, he will crucify Him.

OCTOBER 27

Learning comes from books; penetration of a mystery from suffering.

OCTOBER 28

Skepticism is never certain of itself, being less a firm intellectual position than a pose to justify bad behavior.

OCTOBER 29

There are angels near you to guide you and protect you, if you would but invoke them. It is not later than we think, it is a bigger world than we think.

OCTOBER 30

There is a tendency among many shallow thinkers of our day to teach that every human act is a reflex, over which we do not exercise human control. They would rate a generous deed as no more praiseworthy than a wink, a crime as no more voluntary than a sneeze. . . Such a philosophy undercuts all human dignity. . . All of us have the power of choice in action at every moment of our lives.

OCTOBER 31

In every friendship hearts grow and entwine themselves together, so that the two hearts seem to
make only one heart with only a common thought.
That is why separation is so painful; it is not so much
two hearts separating, but one being torn asunder.

NOVEMBER

NOVEMBER 1

If we wish to have the light, we must keep the sun; if we wish to keep our forests we must keep our trees; if we wish to keep our perfumes, we must keep our flowers—and if we wish to keep our rights, then we must keep our God.

NOVEMBER 2

We can think of Lent as a time to eradicate evil or cultivate virtue, a time to pull up weeds or to plant good seeds. Which is better is clear, for the Christian ideal is always positive rather than negative.

NOVEMBER 3

Unless souls are saved, nothing is saved; there can be no world peace without soul peace.

NOVEMBER 4

Pride is an admission of weakness; it secretly fears all competition and dreads all rivals.

NOVEMBER 5

The better we become, the less conscious we are of our goodness. If anyone admits to being a saint, he is close to being a devil . . . The more saintly we become, the less conscious we are of being holy. A child is cute as long as he does not know he is cute. As soon as he thinks he is, he is a brat. True goodness is unconscious.

NOVEMBER 6

The world is in a state of mortal sin, and it needs absolution. Vain platitudes and 'regeneration,' 'the Constitution' and 'progress' are not going to save us, even though we go on shouting them louder and louder. We need a new word in our vocabulary and that word is: God.

NOVEMBER 7

If a ship is sailing on a polluted canal and wishes to transfer itself to clear waters on a higher level, it must pass through a device which locks out the polluted waters and raises the ship to the higher position. Mary's Immaculate Conception was like that lock . . . [T]hrough her, humanity passed from the lower level of the sons of Adam to the higher level of the sons of God.

NOVEMBER 8

The fact is: you want to be perfectly happy, but you are not. Your life has been a series of disappointments, shocks, and disillusionments. How have you reacted to your disappointments? Either you became cynical or else you became religious.

NOVEMBER 9

Our enjoyment of life is vastly increased if we follow the spiritual injunction to bring some mortification and self-denial into our lives.

NOVEMBER 10

Happiness must be our bridesmaid, not our bride.

NOVEMBER 11

Even friendships are matured in silence. Friends are made by words, love is preserved in silence. The best friends are those who know how to keep the same silences.

NOVEMBER 12

The rapidity of communication, the hourly news broadcasts, tomorrow's news the night before—all these make people live on the surfaces of their souls. The result is that very few live inside themselves. They have their moods determined by the world.

NOVEMBER 13

Never before have men possessed so many time-saving devices. Never before have they had so little time for leisure or repose. Yet few of them are aware of this: advertising has created in modern minds the false notion that leisure and not working are the same-that the more we are surrounded by bolds and wheels, switches and gadgets, the more time we have conquered for our own.

NOVEMBER 14

Repose-true leisure cannot be enjoyed without some recognition of the spiritual world, for the first purpose of repose is the contemplation of the good.

NOVEMBER 15

The egotist, standing alone in his self-imagined greatness, lives in the world of a lie, because the truth about himself would puncture his self-inflation.

NOVEMBER 16

Humility is the pathway to knowledge. No scientist would ever learn the secrets of the atom if, in his conceit, he told the atom what he thought it ought to do. Knowledge comes only with humility before the object which can bring us truth.

NOVEMBER 17

Our modern world has produced a generation of rich politicians who talk love of the poor, but never prove it in action, and a brood of the poor whose hearts are filled with envy for the rich and covetousness of their money.

NOVEMBER 18

External circumstances may condition our mental outlook and our dispositions, but they do not cause them.

NOVEMBER 19

He was lonely, until he found God.

NOVEMBER 20

The more materialistic a civilization is, the more it is in a hurry.

NOVEMBER 21

Satan may appear in many disguises like Christ, and at the end of the world will appear as a benefactor and philanthropist—but Satan never has and never will appear with scars.

NOVEMBER 22

The principle cause of discontent is egotism, or selfishness, which sets the self up as a primary plant around which everyone else must revolve. The second cause of discontent is envy, which makes us regard the possessions and the talents of others as if they were stolen from us The third cause is covetousness, or an inordinate desire to have more, in order to compensate for the emptiness of our heart. The fourth cause of discontent is jealousy, which is sometimes occasioned through melancholia and sadness, and at other times by hatred of those who have what we wish for ourselves.

NOVEMBER 23

What we over-love, we often over-grieve.

NOVEMBER 24

Because we live in a world where position is determined economically, we forget that in God's world the royalty are those who do His will.

NOVEMBER 25

It is typically American to feel that we are not doing anything unless we are doing something big. But from the Chrisian point of view, there is no one thing that is bigger than any other thing.

NOVEMBER 26

A Catholic may sin and sin as badly as anyone else, but no genuine Catholic ever denies he is a sinner. A Catholic wants his sins forgiven—not excused or sublimated.

NOVEMBER 27

Judge the Catholic Church not by those who barely live by its spirit, but by the example of those who live closest to it.

NOVEMBER 28

But when finally the scrolls of history are complete, down to the last word of time, the saddest line of all will be: "There was no room in the inn."The inn was the gathering place of public opinion, the focal point of the world's moods, the rendezvous of the worldly, the rallying place of the popular and the successful. But there's no room in the place where the world gathers. The stable is a place for outcasts, the ignored and the forgotten.

NOVEMBER 29

The world might have expected the Son of God to be born in an inn; a stable would certainly be the last place in the world where one would look for him. The lesson is: divinity is always where you least expect to find it. So the Son of God made man, is invited to enter into his own world through a back door.

NOVEMBER 30

As the "no" of Eve proves that the creature was made by love and is therefore free, so [Mary's] Fiat proves that the Creature was made for love as well.

DECEMBER

DECEMBER 1

Deep sorrow does not come because one has violated a law, but only if one knows he has broken off the relationship with Divine Love.

DECEMBER 2

It is a characteristic of any decaying civilization that the great masses of the people are unconscious of the tragedy. Humanity in a crisis is generally insensitive to the gravity of the times in which it lives. Men do not want to believe their own times are wicked, partly because it involves too much self-accusation and principally because they have no standards outside of themselves by which to measure their times.

DECEMBER 3

But in a conflict between truth and darkness, truth cannot lose.

DECEMBER 4

Evil may have its hour, but God will have His day.

DECEMBER 5

The Rosary is the best therapy for these distraught, unhappy, fearful, and frustrated souls, precisely because it involves the simultaneous use of three powers: the physical, the vocal, and the spiritual, and in that order.

DECEMBER 6

It is not particularly difficult to find thousands who will spend two or three hours a day in exercising, but if you ask them to bend their knees to God in five minutes of prayer they protest that it is too long.

DECEMBER 7

I wonder maybe if our Lord does not suffer more from our indifference, than He did from the crucifixion.

DECEMBER 8

Every earthly ideal is lost by being possessed. The more material your ideal, the greater the disappointment; the more spiritual it is, the less the disillusionment.

DECEMBER 9

Change your entire point of view! Life is not a mockery. Disappointments are merely markers on the road of life, saying: "Perfect happiness is not here." Though your passions may have been satisfied, you were never satisfied, because while your passions can find satisfaction in this world, you cannot.

DECEMBER 10

Many people make the great mistake of aiming directly at pleasure; they forget that pleasure comes only from the fulfillment of a duty or obedience to a law—for man is made to obey the laws of his own nature as inescapably as he must obey the laws of gravity. A boy has pleasure eating ice-cream because he is fulfilling one of the "oughts" of human nature: eating. If he eats more ice-cream that the laws of his body sanction, he will no longer get the pleasure he seeks, but the pain of a stomachache.

To seek pleasure, regardless of law, is to miss it.

DECEMBER 11

(Repose) reminds us that all actions get their worth from God: "Worship" means "admitting worth." To worship is to restore to our workaday life its true worth by setting it in its real relationship to God, Who is its end and ours.

DECEMBER 12

The world blesses not the meek, but the vindictive; it praises not the one who turns the other cheek, but the one who renders evil for evil; it exalts not the humble, but the aggressive. Ideological forces have carried that spirit of violence, class-struggle, and the clenched fist to an extreme the like of which the world before has never seen.

DECEMBER 13

Any book which inspires us to lead a better life is a good book.

DECEMBER 14

Very few people believe in the devil these days, which suits the devil very well. He is always helping to circulate the news of his own death. The essence of God is existence, and He defines Himself as: 'I am Who am.' The essence of the devil is the lie, and he defines himself as: 'I am who am not.' Satan has very little trouble with those who do not believe in him; they are already on his side.

DECEMBER 15

If the bringing of children into the world is today an economic burden, it is because the social system is inadequate; and not because God's law is wrong. Therefore the State should remove the causes of that burden. The human must not be limited and controlled to fit the economic, but the economic must be expanded to fit the human.

DECEMBER 16

The modern atheist does not disbelieve because of his intellect, but because of his will; it is not knowledge that makes him an atheist . . . The denial of God springs from a man's desire not to have a God—from his wish that there were no Justice behind the universe, so that his injustices would fear not retribution; from his desire that there be no Law, so that he may not be judged by it; from his wish that there were no Absolute Goodness, that he might go on sinning with impunity. That is why the modern atheist is always angered when he hears anything said about God and religion—he would be incapable of such a resentment if God were only a myth.

DECEMBER 17

When you think of the condition the world is in now you sometimes wish that Noah had missed the boat.

DECEMBER 18

If I were not a Catholic, and were looking for the true Church in the world today, I would look for the one Church which did not get along well with the world; in other words, I would look for the Church which the world hates. My reason for doing this would be, that if Christ is in any one of the churches of the world today, He must still be hated as He was when He was on earth in the flesh. If you would find Christ today, then find the Church that does not get along with the world.

DECEMBER 19

Look for the Church that is hated by the world, as Christ was hated by the world. Look for the Church which is accused of being behind the times, as Our Lord was accused of being ignorant and never having learned. Look for the Church which men sneer at as socially inferior, as they sneered at Our Lord because He came from Nazareth . . . Look for the Church which the world rejects because it claims it is infallible, as Pilate rejected Christ because he called Himself the Truth. Look for the Church which amid the confusion of conflicting opinions, its members love as they love Christ, and respect its voice as the very voice of its Founder, and the suspicion will grow, that if the Church is unpopular with the spirit of the world, then it is unworldly, and if it is unworldly, it is other-worldly. Since it is other-worldly, it is infinitely loved and infinitely hated as was Christ Himself.

DECEMBER 20

The nice people do not come to God, because they think they are good through their own merits or bad through inherited instincts. If they do good, they believe they are to receive the credit for it; if they do evil, they deny that it is their own fault. They are good through their own good-heartedness, they say; but they are bad because they are misfortunate, either in their economic life or through an inheritance of evil genes from their grandparents.

DECEMBER 21

The nice people rarely come to God; they take their moral tone from the society in which they live. Like the Pharisee in front of the temple, they believe themselves to be very respectable citizens. Elegance is their test of virtue; to them, the moral is the aesthetic, the evil is the ugly. Every move they make is dictated, not by a love of goodness, but by the influence of their age. Their intellects are cultivated—in knowledge of current events; they read only the bestsellers, but their hearts are undisciplined. They say that they would go to church if the Church were only better—but they never tell you how much better the Church must be before they will join it. They sometimes condemn the gross sins of society, such as murder; they are not tempted to these because they fear the opprobrium which comes to them who commit them. By avoiding the sins which society condemns, they escape reproach, they consider themselves good par excellence.

DECEMBER 22

The very freedom which the sinner supposedly exercises in his self-indulgence is only another proof that he is ruled by the tyrant.

DECEMBER 23

There has been no single influence which has done more to prevent man from finding God and rebuilding his character, has done more to lower the moral tone of society than the denial of personal guilt. This repudiation of man's personal responsibility for his action is falsely justified in two ways: by assuming that man is only an animal and by giving a sense of guilt the tag "morbid."

DECEMBER 24

What is discovered may be abused, but that does not mean the discovery was evil.

DECEMBER 25

It is not the sanctuary that is in danger; it is civilization. It is not infallibility that may go down; it is personal rights. It is not the Eucharist that may pass away; it is freedom of conscience. It is not divine justice that may evaporate; it is the courts of human justice. It is not that God may be driven from His throne; it is that men may lose the meaning of home; For peace on earth will come only to those who give glory to God! It is not the Church that is in danger, it is the world!

DECEMBER 26

Many a modern preacher is far less concerned with preaching Christ and Him crucified than he is with his popularity with his congregation.

DECEMBER 27

Since evil is nothing positive, there can be no principle of evil. It has no meaning expect in reference to something good.

DECEMBER 28

We are living in perilous times when the hearts and souls of men are sorely tried. Never before has the future been so utterly unpredictable; we are not so much in a period of transition with belief in progress to push us on, rather we seem to be entering the realm of the unknown, joylessly, disillusioned, and without hope. The whole world seems to be in a state of spiritual widowhood, possessed of the harrowing devastation of one who set out on life's course joyously in intimate comradeship with another, and then is bereft of that companion forever.

DECEMBER 29

Our Lord was born not just of her flesh but also by her consent.

DECEMBER 30

The life of a bishop should be more perfect than the life of a hermit. The reason he gave was that the holiness which the monk preserves in the desert must be preserved by the bishop into the midst of the evil of the world.

DECEMBER 31

With the crib seen as a tabernacle and the child as a kind of host, then the home becomes a living temple of God. The sacristan of that sanctuary is the mother, who never permits the tabernacle lamp of faith to go out.

Can someone who has been broken,
be healed & become more beautiful
than ever before?

"*I am so excited for you!*

This book changed my life. If you only buy one book
this year . . . get yourself a copy of *Ask Him!*"

- MATTHEW KELLY